KU-428-350

FOREWORD

There is nothing like a really wet game for having some good clean fun!

This book contains a selection of watery games aimed at all ages - from the young to the young at heart. Ideal for livening up a camp, holiday or a sunny afternoon in a garden or park, these games often need little equipment other than a good supply of fresh water.

For those not used to running games for young people, unaccustomed to venturing out of a meeting hall - or simply shy and reserved, I have noted down a few pearls of wisdom to assist in running games.

The games that follow have all been tried and tested by the members of the 15th Ealing Scout Group in West London and are all guaranteed to be great fun! I am therefore indebted to the young members in the Group for putting up with me as I tried out these games - and I apologise to them for inflicting upon them those which did not work and did not, as a result, make it into the book.

I am also grateful to Emma for her encouragement - and for telling me patiently that some of my more weird and wonderful ideas should not even be tested, let alone printed.

Have fun!

DAVE WOOD

INDEX

GAMES WITH WATER-FILLED BALLOONS

SAFETY FIRST

If playing games <u>with</u> water, remember that some young people simply do not like getting their faces wet. Make sure that all players understand what is involved before you start the game, as there is nothing worse than having someone upset during what should be a fun activity. These youngsters could be given jobs as scorers or marshals, to keep them part of the group.

If playing games <u>in</u> water, you must make sure that you have enough lifeguards (who can actually swim!) to look after your group. These adults should stand around the water's edge, not in the water. Make sure that the game or activity does not develop into horseplay, as this can quickly get out of hand and could lead to injury.

Games <u>in</u> water should only be played in shallow water, preferably no more than waist-deep. Never play games in a river or canal or where there may be underwater obstructions or currents.

GAMES WITH WATER PISTOLS

Water pistols can be great fun - not just for a water fight but for games which involve skill and a steady hand. For many of the games printed here hand sprayers normally used for spraying houseplants are even better than water pistols. These are often very cheap and easy to find in garden centres and hardware stores. Alternatively, old washing-up liquid bottles are often great to use, although the water tends to come out too quickly from them. Be sure to wash these bottles our thoroughly before use.

Excellent water pistols can be made using large plastic soft drinks bottles by simply piercing a small hole in the lid. The lid will not fly off in use, unlike most washing-up liquid bottles, and can hold a healthy supply of water.

GAMES WITH BLINDFOLDS

Some games require the use of blindfolds. Traditional ones are seldom 100 per cent effective and are usually awkward to tie securely. Far better, then, to invest in a few cheap pairs of swimming goggles. Cover the <u>outside</u> of the clear plastic with black paint, using two or three coats if necessary. These can be instantly put on and removed by the players and will seldom allow visibility. Always have sufficient help on hand to ensure safety when playing any sort of games involving blindfolds.

BEING OUT

It is not fun being 'out' during a game, having to watch the remaining players enjoying themselves. This is easily avoided by awarding players penalty points instead of making them 'out'. Thus, at the end of the give time, those players with the least penalty points are the winners.

CO-OPERATIVE GAMES

Whilst the majority of the games in this book have been written with a competitive aim, they could easily be turned into co-operative games with only slight alterations.

LEADING GAMES

- Choose the right game for the right occasion.
- Never over use any particular game.
- Name the game, to help the players remember which ones they like.
- Change the name of a game to suit whatever theme might be appropriate. This will aid the players' enjoyment.
- Ensure you have the required equipment to hand before starting the game.
- Be clear as to how you want the players - standing, sitting, relay form, two equal teams, etc.
- Know the game thoroughly before teaching it - avoid reading instructions from a book.
- Modify games as appropriate to allow for handicapped participants or special circumstances.
- Run through a game using one or two players before actually starting it.
- Explain the rules clearly and as concisely as possible, once the players are in position. Do not embellish the rules unnecessarily.

- Avoid the use of a whistle to obtain quiet - personality and hand signals should be all that are required.
- Ask for any questions before you start the game.
- Be enthusiastic in leading the games and this will brush off on the players.
- Ensure silence whilst teaching the game, but encourage noise whilst playing it.
- Do not encourage cheating, nor let it go unchecked, even if only due to over-enthusiasm.
- Always remember the safety and happiness of the players.
- Do not let a game drag on, nor play it more than twice in succession.
- If a game is not working, stop it, re-explain the rules and start again.
- Ensure that the players know the boundary lines before starting a game.
- If equal teams are needed, let the first player in a team with short numbers go twice. Avoid making an odd player drop out.
- Take part in the games yourself from time to time - but only to show that you are game for a laugh. Never participate just to show off.

0 - HOLE IN ONE

Number of players: Any.
You will need: toilet tissue, water pistols, string and sticky tape.
The game:
A strip of tissue is hung from a line (weight the bottom by taping a stick to it) and players take it in turns to see how quickly they can force a hole in the paper using a water pistol. This could be run as a relay or with pairs of players seeing who is the quickest. The distance players stand from the paper depends on how powerful the water pistol is and how soft, strong ('.....and very very long', etc) the paper is - experiment before you start the game to see the best distance.

1 - SITTING DUCKS

Number of players: Any.
You will need: Water pistols, a table, a plank of wood and about six to ten plastic ducks.
The game:
The plank is put on its edge on the table top and the ducks are lined up along the uppermost edge of the plank as shown. Two players face each other, either side of the table, and each holds a water pistol. On the word 'go', they must try to shoot the ducks off the plank onto their opponent's side of the table. You may need to erect a string line which players must not cross, depending on how powerful your water pistols are. The winner is the player who has the least ducks on his or her side of the plank. The drenching of an opponent is, of course, permitted in order to put them off - but avoid squirting the eyes.

2 - HEAD WAITERS

Number of players: Any, in as many equal teams as appropriate.

You will need: For each team - a bowl of water, an empty bucket and one plastic disposable cup.

The game:

Players line up in relay formation, with their bowl of water at the front of the line. Some distance in front of each team is their empty bucket. On the word 'go', the first player in each team fills the cup with water and places it on his or her head. They are allowed to use only one hand to steady the cup and must race to their bucket, where they empty what water is left in the cup and run back to let the second player go. When all have run, or after a given time limit (say, four minutes), the winning team is that with the most water in its bucket. Advanced players could use Version Two of this game, where both hands are held behind the runner's back, balancing the cup on the head unaided.

3 - KEEP IT UP

Number of players: Any, in relay form or in pairs.

You will need: Balloons, two water pistols.

The game:

Two players are given an inflated balloon each and a water pistol. On the word 'go', they must throw their balloon in the air and keep it up whilst walking over a short course. The winner is the first to get back to the start. If a balloon hits the ground, the player must stop and push it back into the air and continue along the course. Umbrellas are a useful aid, but should not be permitted.

4 - TO AND FRO

Number of players: Any, in two teams of roughly equal numbers.
You will need: Balloons and water pistols/washing-up liquid bottles.
The game:
Players sit cross-legged in their teams, in two lines about two metres apart, and with the two teams facing each other. Each player has some form of water pistol. The inflated balloon is thrown into the middle of the playing area and the players must shoot water at it in order to get it to hit a player on the opposing team, thus scoring a goal. Players must not move nor get up and may not refill until a goal has been scored. See which team is the first to reach five goals. Speed the game up by using more than one balloon!

5 - SOFTLY, SOFTLY

Number of players: Any.
You will need: A water-filled washing-up liquid bottle (or similar) and a plastic cup of water.
The game:
Players are seated in a large circle, in the middle of which sits a player chosen at random. This player is the Guardian of the Water and is blindfolded. The cup of water is placed on the ground just in front of the Guardian, who is armed with the washing-up liquid bottle. A player from the circle is chosen at random to try and creep up to the Guardian and grab the cup of water. If the Guardian hears the person approaching, he or she may try to squirt the attacker with water from the bottle. If the attacker is hit, he or she returns to the circle and a new attacker is chosen. If the attacker makes it to the cup without getting squirted, he or she should pick up the cup and empty it over the Guardian's head! This game is, of course, ideal for the outdoors, but also is great fun when played indoors at the end of a club meeting - but do not forget to mop the water up afterwards.

15

6 - SPANISH WAITERS

Number of players: Any, in two equal teams.
You will need: Several bowls of water, an empty bucket, several sponges, four plastic cups and a tray.
The game:
Team A divides itself into two and stands in two lines, about 3 metres apart, facing inwards. The bowl of water is placed two or three metres away from one end of the divide, with the empty bucket the same distance from the other end, as illustrated. On the word 'go', the players in team B take it in turns, relay-style, to fill the four cups with water, place them on the tray and run between the two lines of the other team to the other end, where they deposit what water they still have in the bucket and run back to tag the next 'waiter'. Meanwhile, team A is armed with water-filled sponges and must try to knock the cups off the tray. The game continues until all waiters have had a turn and the water collected in the bucket is measured. Teams then swap round and repeat the above.

7 - THE FOUNTAIN OF YOUTH

Number of players: Any, in roughly equal teams.
You will need: An empty bowl or bucket per team, a supply of plastic cups and a fairly powerful hose, fitted with some form of sprinkler (and attached to the mains).
The game:
The hose is attached to a stake in such a way that it points into the air and, when the water is turned on, a fountain of water sprays over as wide an area as possible. Players sit in relay form about ten metres from the 'waterfall', with the empty bowl and cup at the front of each team. On the word 'Go', the first player in each team grabs their cup and runs to the waterfall where they must collect as much water in their cup as possible. A whistle is blown after a short time (say, 30-45 seconds) and these players must stop collecting water and return to their teams, emptying the cup into their bowl. Player two from each team takes the cup, runs up and collects more water until the whistle is blown again and so on, until each player has had at least two turns. The team with the greatest collection of water (in the bowl, not in their clothes!) at the end is the winner.

8 - HEAD CASES

Number of players: Any, in equal teams.
You will need: A large supply of balloons (see below), partially-filled with water, string and one 'headpiece' per team, as described below.
The game:
Perhaps using a tree or a sturdy washing line (or similar), you will need to string up the balloons - ideally having two balloons per player and, if possible, having a different colour balloon for each team. Teams sit in relay form about ten metres away from the balloons, with the headpiece in the hands of player one. On the word 'Go', player one puts the headpiece on and runs to the balloons, where he or she must try to burst ONE balloon. When this has been done, the players return to their teams, hand the headpieces to the next in line who must run up and repeat the process.

9 - WATER CATCH

Number of players: Any, in pairs.
You will need: A supply of balloons, each filled with as much water as possible.
The game:
Players face each other and stand about one metre apart. One player gently throws the balloon to his or her partner, who catches it and takes a step backwards before throwing it back carefully to the first player. This continues, with each player taking a step backwards between throws until someone drops the balloon. See how far apart they can go successfully without getting wet feet!

10 - BARMY BALLOON BUNG

Number of players: At least ten, in two equal teams.
You will need: A supply of balloons, partly-filled with water.
The game:
Each team chooses a player to be the 'catcher', who stands on a chair behind the opposing team, as indicated below. On the starting whistle, a balloon is thrown into the centre of the playing area and teams must attempt to pass it to their catcher. A goal is scored for every successful catch. Players may not run with the balloon, nor may there by any physical contact. Depending on the enthusiasm of the players, deliberate bursting of the balloon may need to result in a goal automatically being scored against the offender's team. After a goal, the balloon is returned to the referee who starts the game again.

11 - BALLOONY-BALL

Number of players: Any, in two equal teams.
You will need: A supply of balloons partly filled with water and a volleyball net (real or home-made).
The game:
This game is played as per volleyball, but with much less talent and finesse. Players simply attempt to hit the balloon over the net. If the balloon bursts or hits the ground, the team on whose side this has happened loses a point from a starting total of, say, ten. Keep playing until one team has lost all of its points or until teatime, whichever is soonest.

12 - CHANGE BALLOON BUNG

Number of players: At least ten, in two equal teams.
You will need: A supply of balloons, partly-filled with water.
The game:
This is a variation of BARMY BALLOON BUNG, with the exception that the two catchers do not represent either team. The game commences as before until the referee shouts 'CHANGE'. Teams must then immediately change the direction in which they are playing and try to get the balloon to the catcher at the opposite end of the playing area. To lessen the confusion, one team's players could be identified with scarves around their necks. The referee would hold a scarf in the hand closest to that team's goal. Thus, when the referee shouts 'CHANGE', the scarf is passed into the other hand to help remind the teams in which direction they are now playing.

13 - CORKO

Number of players: Any, in equal teams.
You will need: For each team - a cork, plastic washing-up liquid bottle and a supply of water.
The game:
Teams line up in relay formation, with the first in each line holding the water-filled bottle and with the cork lying on the ground. On the word 'Go', these players must propel their cork to a given point some five metres away, by squirting water from the bottle at the cork. Once at the given point, players should pick the cork up and run back to their team to set the next player off. Bottles may be recharged at any time, but the cork must be stationary when this is being done. Speed the game up by having two bottles per team - one in use and one being refilled.

14 - CUP 'O' BUNDLE

Number of players: Any, in two equal teams.
You will need: A small supply of water, one or two plastic cups, two chairs and four bean bags (or similar).
The game:
Teams sit facing each other in two lines, approximately three or four metres apart, with a chair placed at either end in the middle of the lines and about six metres apart. The four bean bags and a cup of water are placed in the centre of the playing area. The players are numbered off and the leader then calls a number at random. The two players with that number run to the centre, grab one bean bag each and run to place it on their team's chair before running back to grab a second bag. When a player has two bean bags on his or her chair, they may grab the cup and throw the water over their opponent. The cup is refilled, the bags replaced and another number is called. There is no need to keep a score, as there will be enough fun just watching the action.

15 - RUNNING SHOWER

<u>Number of players</u>: Any, in equal teams.
<u>You will need</u>: For each team - an empty bowl, one doctored bucket on a stick, as shown below, plus a good supply of water.
<u>The game</u>:
Teams line up in relay formation, facing their empty bowl placed some distance away (12-15m). Each has a doctored bucket and, on the word 'go' must fill it with water and carry it aloft to their bowl, into which they deposit what water they have left in their bucket. When each player has had a turn, the accumulated water is measured and the team with the most water is the winner.

16 - TRAIL LAYING

Number of players: Six, in two teams of three.
You will need: Three water pistols/old washing-up liquid bottles.
The game:
One team sets off around a park or other suitable playing area, each player carrying a water pistol. They use these to 'write' tracking signs (arrows and crosses) on the ground in water. Ten minutes after they have set off, the other team sets off and must follow the trail before the signs dry. Arrange a final meeting point (just in case the trackers are not quick enough!) and swap round. You could use ice cubes if playing the game around fields and woodland, where water would not show.

17 - HUMAN TABLES

Number of players: Any, in small teams of roughly equal number.
You will need: A large supply of paper or plastic (disposable) cups, a supply of water for each team and a measuring jug.
The game:
Working in their teams, one player is chosen to be the 'table' and must kneel down with their hands on the ground, so that their back forms a fairly flat, level surface. On the word 'Go', the team members fill the cups with water and place them carefully onto their 'human table'. Teams are given a set time, say, two minutes, to place as many water-filled cups as possible onto their table. At the end of this time, a whistle is blown and the amount of water still in cups on each team's table is measured - that with the most water being declared the winner. Note: it is almost imposible to be a dry table if one is prone to fits of the giggles or coughing attacks, so players should, perhaps, choose their tables wisely.

18 - GOOD DOGGY

Number of players: Any, in equal teams.
You will need: A bowl of water, an empty bowl and a clean sponge per team.
The game:
Teams line up in relay form, with a bowl of water containing the bath sponge in front of them. About ten metres in front of each team is an empty bowl. On the word 'Go', the first player in each team must, without the use of hands, pick their sponge up in their teeth, stand up and run to their team's empty bowl, where they can use their hands to squeeze into the bowl what water remains. They then run back to their teams and place the sponge in the full bowl for the next player to have a turn. After a given time, say, four minutes, the team with the most water at the far end is the winner.

19 - APPLE SCRUMPING

Number of players: Any.
You will need: One or more apples/bean bags, a number of plastic cups and a supply of water.
The game:
The players sit in a large circle, and an apple (or beanbag) is placed in the centre. One player is chosen to be the 'scrumper' and must move away from the circle, so that he or she can not see any of the other players. Five players around the circle are chosen at random and are each given a cup of water, and one of these players is chosen to be the 'farmer' who must guard the 'orchard' - the farmer's identity must be unknown to the scrumper. The scrumper returns and must try to grab the apple and get it outside the circle without being 'caught' by the farmer. The farmer catches the scrumper by throwing the cup of water over him or her - the other players with cups are there simply to confuse the scrumper. The farmer is not allowed to move until the apple has been actually touched and the scrumper must leave the circle at exactly the same point through which he or she entered. The scrumper who gets the apple outside the circle wins and could eat the apple, perhaps, as their prize.

20 - WATER OBSTACLE

Number of players: Any, in two or more equal teams.
You will need: A plastic mug (with a handle), a supply of water, a ball of fairly tough string (such as sisal) and an empty bucket.
The game:
An obstacle course is set up, using tables, chairs, planks and trees, and the string is laid along the length of the course. It is secured at both ends to tent pegs firmly embedded in the ground after threading through the handle of the mug. The string should thread over, under and through the obstacles as appropriate. One team is chosen and on the word 'go', the first player in this team fills the mug with water and completes the obstacle course, mug in hand. The remaining water in the mug is emptied into the bucket to be measured later, and the player must run back through the course (with the mug) to set the second player off. When each player has had a turn, the water collected is measured and team two has its go.

21 - FIRE FIGHTER

Number of players: Any
You will need: Candles, matches and water pistols.
The game:
Each player tries to extinguish a lighted candle using a water pistol. Play this against the clock or in pairs - and have plenty of spare candles ready for all to have a go.

22 - FIFTEEN PASSES

Number of players: Any, in two equal teams.
You will need: A supply of balloons, partly filled with water.
The game:
A playing area is defined and the balloon is thrown into play. Teams must attempt to pass it amongst their own players 15 times. There must be no physical contact as teams attempt to intercept the balloon and players must not run with the balloon. If it is dropped, or if it bursts (and is replaced), the counting must start again.

23 - HOT EGGS

<u>Number of players</u>: Ten or more.
<u>You will need</u>: A supply of balloons, <u>half</u>-filled with water.
<u>The game</u>:
Players stand in a big circle (they put their arms out and move outwards until their fingertips just touch those of their neighbours, then drop their arms ready to play) with the leader standing in the centre. A balloon is handed to a player, who passes it in a clockwise direction around the circle. If the balloon bursts or a player drops it, that person (or whoever's 'fault' it was!) is out and sits down where they are. The balloon continues its journey around the circle, being passed over the heads of those who are out to the next person who is standing. Meanwhile (and this is where it gets fun!), the leader has a second balloon and passes it to a player, who must then return it to the leader. Once again, if a player drops or bursts the balloon, he or she is out. The leader can work around the circle clockwise, anti-clockwise or (more successfully) at random.

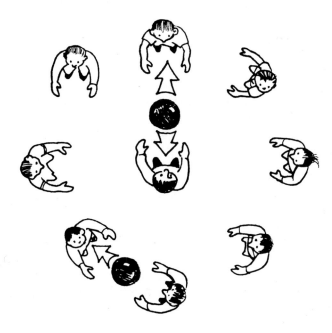

24 - BANGLE BUNGLE

Number of players: Any.
You will need: One balloon partly filled with water per person and some string.
The game:
Each player has a balloon tied to their right wrist with a piece of string, so that there is about half a metre of string between the balloon and the player's hand. A playing area is indicated (in a hall, or outside the corners of a large square marked out) and, on the word 'go', players must attempt to burst the balloon belonging to any of the other players. As soon as a player's balloon has been burst, he or she is out of the game and must stand at the side.

25 - SPOT THE SPONGE

Number of players: Any.
You will need: Three bath sponges and a supply of water.
The game:
Players sit in a large (arms-length) circle, except for one player chosen at random, who stands slightly away from the circle, facing away from it (if played indoors, this player could be outside the room). Those in the circle pass the water-soaked sponges to another player across the circle continuously. The chosen player than counts to three out loud, at whatever gaps between each number. On the word 'three', this player may suddenly turn around and go to the circle, upon which signal, players must try to conceal the sponges without the chosen one seeing their whereabouts - a great test of keeping a straight face whilst sitting on a soggy sponge, perhaps! The chosen one then has three guesses to try and identify which players are holding the sponges. Another player is chosen to leave the circle, the sponges are recharged with water, and the game begins again.

26 - FILL 'EM UP!

<u>Number of players</u>: Any, in three or more equal teams.
<u>You will need</u>: A plastic cup per player and a bucket with a measured amount of water per team.
<u>The game</u>:
Teams sit an equal distance from each other, with their bucket (each containing precisely the same amount of water) sitting in front of them. On the word 'go', players run to opposing teams' buckets, grab a cupful of water and take it back to their own bucket. After a given time, or when complete and utter chaos has broken out, a whistle is sounded and teams gather around their buckets to see who has retained the most water.

27 - WATER FLIGHTS

<u>Number of players</u>: Any, in two equal teams.
<u>You will need</u>: A supply of A4-sized paper, 'water pistols' and/or sponges - plus loads of water!
<u>The game</u>:
Team A line up either side of a three-metre wide strip, whilst Team B's players each make a paper aeroplane. Team A is armed with sponges, water pistols and the like and has a supply of water to hand. Team B players take it in turns to throw their paper aeroplanes along the strip between Team A's players, who must try to hit it with the sponges or water. Team B scores a point for each aircraft, which makes it to a pre-determined finishing line and, when all planes have flown, teams swap around.

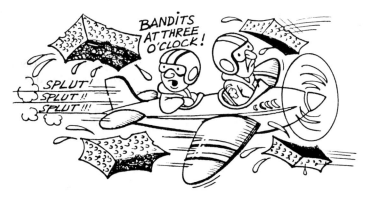

28 - FLAKE-OUT

<u>Number of players</u>: One energetic adult for every three to five youngsters.

<u>You will need</u>: One old coat per adult, plus several balloons partly filled with water.

<u>The game</u>:

About ten balloons are attached to a coat using string and safety pins, and the adult puts the coat on. A playing area is defined and a time limit is set (say, three or four minutes). On the word 'go', the players (no more than five!) must simply try to catch the adult and burst the balloons (the players should not get wetter than the adult, we promise). The adult, not surprisingly, will try not to be caught. At the end of the given time, if any balloon is still intact, the adult has won. If they are all burst, the players have won. Several games could be played at the same time, but with separate playing areas.

29 - ON TARGET

<u>Number of players</u>: Any.

<u>You will need</u>: One washing-up liquid bottle or squeezy drinks bottle per player, water-based felt-tipped pens or poster paint.

<u>The game</u>:

Players must wear swimming costumes for this and draw simple targets or pictures on either their thigh, stomach or chest (depending which is visible!). On the word 'go', players must try to smudge the target or picture on the other players, whilst trying to protect themselves. No physical contact is allowed. There need not be any winners and no one need be out -just see who can retain their artwork intact.

30 - SPIKE IT

Number of players: Any, in equal teams.
You will need: A horizontal line (of rope), suspended between two trees at least four metres above the ground, several balloons half-filled with water, and one pole or bamboo cane per team, with a drawing pin attached to one end as shown below.
The game:
Players sit in relay formation, some distance from the line, from which are suspended the balloons. On the word 'Go', the first player in each team takes the pole, runs to the line, and attempts to burst a balloon. When one is burst, he or she runs back to the team to set the next player off. The first team back, with each player having burst a balloon, is the winner.

31 - HOP 'N' SPLASH

Number of players: Any, in equal teams.
You will need: For each team - a bowl of water, a plastic mug and an empty bucket.
The game:
Teams sit in relay formation with the bowl at the front of the team and the bucket placed some distance away. On the word 'Go', the first player in each team fills the mug with water and hop to the bucket, into which any remaining water in the mug is poured. At the end of the given time (four or five minutes) or when all have had a go, the amount of water collected is measured.

32 - SOGGY ANKLES

Number of players: Any.
You will need: A length of string (sisal is best) and a supply of double balloons (one balloon inserted inside the other before inflating them - this makes them tougher) half filled with water.
The game:
Players stand in a large circle around the leader, who holds one end of the string, on the other end of which is tied a balloon. The balloon is swung around the circle and the players must jump over the string and balloon whenever it comes to them. (The leader gets the balloon swinging round before the players close in the circle to jump over it, otherwise the leader will not be able to swing the balloon at a sufficient speed). If the string catches around anyone's ankles, or if the balloon bursts against a player's feet, that person is out (or loses a 'life') and the game recommences.

33 - LONG SPLASH

Number of players: Any.
You will need: One or more large foam mattresses and a supply of water.
The game:
An ideal activity for a silly sports contest is this. Set up a long jump base, with the mattress(es) positioned lengthwise where the sand would normally be - for safety reasons, if the mattress can be placed on an existing long jump sand pit, so much the better. Just before the activity starts, thoroughly soak the mattress with water - it makes a great (if rather soggy) landing cushion for the players, with onlookers getting fairly damp too! Players take it in turns to see how far they can long jump, with their distances being marked using sticks laid flat on the ground to the side of the landing zone.

34 - KNEE DRENCHING

Number of players: Any, in equal teams.
You will need: A supply of balloons half filled with water, inflated to near bursting point.
The game:
Teams line up in relay formation. On the word 'Go', the first person in each team places the balloon between their knees and hops to a marked line some distance away and back again, without using hands, whereupon the balloon is passed to the next person. If the balloon falls, the player must stop and replace it between the knees. If it bursts, the player must wait until a referee has passed them a replacement balloon. First team whose players have all participated is the winner.

35 - SACK SOAK

Number of players: Any, in two teams.
You will need: A supply of water, one plastic cup per player, two black plastic sacks and a brave (or waterproof) leader.
The game:
The leader holds a sack in each hand and teams are named 'left' and 'right'. The players must try to get as much water in their own sack as possible within the given time. The leader may wander (or run) around the given area and turn around at will. No physical contact is permitted and the game continues for about four or five minutes. The team with the most water in its bag is the winner. Naturally, players might wish to distract their opponents to prevent them filling the sack - this is fine, although pushing and shoving is not permitted.

36 - BOTTLE BOMBING

Number of players: Five to seven.
You will need: Seven (or so) empty washing up bottles/plastic soft drinks bottles, a sponge football and a few bowls of water.
The game:
Two large concentric circles are marked out (the inner being 2m diameter, the outer about 8m) and one player is chosen to stand in the centre circle, along with the five empty bottles. The players stand outside the outer circle and have the sponge ball, which is soaked in water. On the word 'Go', they must pass the ball around (re-soaking it as necessary) and try to knock down the bottles within, say, one and a half minutes. The defender can stand fallen bottles up. At the end of the given time the number of bottles still standing is that player's score. The defender then joins the attackers, one of whom then takes a turn in the centre. The winner is the player who has the highest score when all have had a turn.

37 - CUP CHAOS

Number of players: Any, in equal teams.
You will need: A supply of plastic cups, water and two bowls or buckets per team.
The game:
Players sit in relay formation, with a bowl of water in front of each team, and with the second bowl placed upside down some distance away. On the word 'Go', the first player in each team fills a cup with water, runs to the far end, around their inverted bowl and back, passing the cup to player two. This player will have filled a second cup with water and must complete the course carrying the two cups. The third player carries three cups...and so on. The last player in the team carries all the cups to the inverted bowl and must right it and empty into it what water remains in the cups.

38 - BOLLARDS

<u>Number of players</u>: Any, in two equal teams.
<u>You will need</u>: A large supply of sponges, a good supply of water and one large parking cone per team.
<u>The game</u>:
Two parallel lines are marked, being about three metres apart, with teams standing either side of this 'no man's land', each given a large supply of sponges, soaking in bowls of water. One player from each team holds a cone and stands in amongst the players on the opposing team. On the word 'Go', players must throw the water-filled sponges to their team-mate with the cone, who must attempt to catch as many as possible in the cone. Players may, of course, distract their opponents' aim by throwing the sponges at them. No physical contact is permitted, and each team should have a judge to count the number of sponges caught. Sponges should be removed from the cones from time to time to enable the game to continue for a reasonable period.

39 - SPONGE BUNGEE

<u>Number of players</u>: At least ten, in two equal teams.
<u>You will need</u>: 12 empty washing-up liquid/plastic soft drinks bottles, a supply of water and several sponges.
<u>The game</u>:
Divide the rectangular playing area into two halves, with one team standing in each half. Behind each team, at either end of the playing area, are placed six bottles in a line. On the starting whistle, teams must use the water-soaked sponges to try and knock down the opposing team's bottles. The first team to knock down all of the other team's bottles is the winner, re-soaking sponges as frequently as desired. Bottles must not be righted once they have been knocked down.

40 - FOOT 'N' MOUTH

<u>Number of players</u>: Any, in equal teams.
<u>You will need</u>: A supply of plastic cups, water and two bowls or buckets per team.
<u>The game</u>:
Players sit in relay formation, with a bowl of water at the front of each team. On the word 'Go', the first player in each team fills up a cup with water, holds it in his or her mouth between their teeth, and runs to their second (empty) bowl, placed some distance away. Any water that remains in the cup is emptied into the bowl and the player runs back to set off the next person. When all have had a turn, whichever team has collected the most water is the winner.

41 - CURTAIN BUNG

<u>Number of players</u>: At least six, in two equal teams.
<u>You will need</u>: A large groundsheet or similar. Several balloons half-filled with water.
<u>The game</u>:
A washing line is built, which is around 3m from the ground and from which is suspended a groundsheet or similar. Teams stand either side of the groundsheet. A balloon is thrown over the curtain to the other team, who catch it and throw it back.

42 - BACKWARDS BILLY

<u>Number of Players</u>: Any, in equal teams.
<u>You will need</u>: For each team - a billy (or similar container) and a (measured) bowl of water.
<u>The game</u>:
Players line up in relay form with a bowl of water at the front of each team. On the word 'Go', the first player must grab the billy using both hands <u>behind</u> their back and run to a marked point some five metres away and back again. Once back at their bowl, they must pour what water remains into the bowl. The billy is passed to the next player who repeats the above. When each team has finished, award points for first, second and third, plus the quantity of water remaining in the bowl.

43 - WHOOPS!

<u>Number of players</u>: Any, in equal teams.
<u>You will need</u>: For each team - an empty milk bottle, a bucket of water and a mug.
<u>The game</u>:
Players sit in relay form and three metres in front of each team lies the bucket, bottle and mug. Player 1 stands by the bucket and hold the bottle on his or her head. On the word 'Go', player 2 runs to the bucket and starts to fill the bottle as quickly as possible, with player 1 standing upright all the time. When the bottle is filled, player 1 runs back to tag player 3, whilst player 2 empties the bottle and places it on his or her own head. The first team whose players have all had a turn is the winner - a team of judges may be required to ensure that bottle-holders do not bend over and that bottles are filled (and emptied!) correctly.

44 - CANDLE DOUSING

Number of players: Any, in two equal teams.
You will need: For each team - a candle in a jar, a supply of water, plastic cups and a selection of 'water pistols'.
The game:
Teams base their lighted candle in a suitable location at either end of a large playing area, such as a field. There is a central water supply (supervised by a leader) and each player has a plastic cup and/or some form of water pistol. On the starting whistle, teams attempt to douse the opposing team's candle, whilst defending their own. Candles may not be blown out - a supervisor may be required at each base to ensure that the Geneva Convention is followed at all times! Once a player has run out of water, he or she may return to the water supply and refill. Spare candles and plastic cups may be required for future rounds of this action-packed game.

45 - BUCKET HEAD

Number of players: Any, in two equal teams.
You will need: A 'bucket head' device for each team, as illustrated opposite, about 25 clothes pegs per team and a supply of plastic cups and water.
The game:
One player from each team wears the bucket head and also has the clothes pegs attached to his or her clothing. Each team's pegs should be marked with a different colour. On the word 'Go', players must try to fill their own team mate's bucket by throwing cups of water into it. At the same time, players must try to remove all of the clothes pegs from the opposing catcher. When one team has removed all of the opposing team's pegs, the amount of water collected is measured and a winner announced.

46 - FOOL BUNG

Number of players: At least ten.
You will need: Several balloons more than half filled with water, inflated to near bursting point.
The game:
Players form a large circle with their arms held behind their (own) backs. The leader stands in the centre of the circle, holding a balloon. The leader tries to fool the players by pretending to throw the balloon to them and, if players react as if to catch it, they are out and must sit down. If the balloon bursts on a player, they are also out and must sit down.

47 - MALLET MESS

Number of players: Any, in equal teams.
You will need: For each team - a mallet, blindfold and a supply of balloons half filled with water.
The game:
Teams sit in relay form and, on the word 'Go', the first player in each dons the blindfold, takes the mallet and crawls to a point about four metres away, where their team's balloon lies. This player must find the balloon (shouted instructions from team mates may be needed) and burst it using the mallet. Upon doing so, the blindfold is removed and the player returns to set the next person off to burst a new balloon, and so on.

48 - SHEET SHAMBLES

Number of players: Any, in teams of about four or five.
You will need: For each team - a sheet of plastic and a measured bucketful of water.
The game:
Teams must hold their plastic sheeting whilst their measured bucketful of water is poured into it. A route is described around a field, woodland or wherever (including a few chicanes and other tight squeezes or awkward obstacles if possible) and, on the word 'Go', teams race around the course. Teams win points for their finishing position and for the quantity of water remaining in their sheet.

49 - BLINDFOLD BUNDLE

Number of players: Any, in two equal teams.
You will need: A large supply of balloons (half of which are round, half long), half filled with water, and a blindfold for each player.
The game:
Teams are allocated a shape of balloon. These are placed in the centre of the playing area. On the word 'Go', players crawl to the balloon and try to burst their team's balloons. They must not use feet or hands to burst the balloons (nor pins, pointed sticks or axes). First team to have burst all of its balloons is the winner.

50 - MALTESER DUNKING

Number of players: Any, in equal teams.
You will need: For each team - a bowl of water and a packet of Maltesers.
The game:
Players sit in relay form, with a bowl of water about five metres in front of each team. The Maltesers are poured into the water, on which they float (put them in the water just prior to the game, or they may go soggy). On the word 'Go', the first players in each team race to the bowl and, with hands behind their backs, attempt to grab one sweet with their teeth. Upon doing so, they run back to set the next player off. First team whose players have all eaten a sweet is the winner.

51 - JELLY DUNKING

Number of players: Any, in equal teams.
You will need: For each team - a bowl of water and a packet of jelly babies.
The game:
This is played exactly as MALTESER DUNKING, but since the jelly babies sink and become slippery, it is a much wetter game.

52 - BASEBALL-OON

Number of players: Any.
You will need: A baseball, rounders or cricket bat plus a supply of balloons, partly filled with water.
The game:
This makes a good base in an obstacle course and is great fun whilst getting the player fairly wet. The player approaches the given point in the course, picks up the bat and has to hit three balloons (or just one, as you wish) bursting them as they are thrown to him or her. Score one point for each balloon burst by holding the bat in the air.

53 - SUBMARINES

Number of players: Any, in two equal teams.
You will need: Half the number of blindfolds, plastic cups and buckets of water than there are players.
The game:
The players in Team A are the submarines and are blindfold, sitting at random in the middle of the playing area and facing any direction. Each of these players has a cup and a bucket of water. The leader chooses individual members of Team B to be ships, who try to sneak through the blindfold players to a marked safety zone beyond them. If the submarines think they can hear an approaching player, they may throw a cupful of water in that direction. If hit by water, an 'attacker' sits down and becomes an extra obstacle. If submarines get hit by water - too bad! Swap the teams around once all attackers have had to go - the winning team is that which has the greatest number of ships through to the safe zone unscathed.

54 - SPONGE ROUNDERS

Number of players: Any, in two equal teams.
You will need: A rounders bat (or similar), posts, a sponge and a bucket of water.
The game:
This is played exactly as normal rounders (whatever your local rules might be), with the ball replaced by a soggy sponge. The sponge is resoaked by the bowler at every opportunity, using the bucket of water which marks the bowler's base.

55 - WATERBARROWS

Number of players: Any, in equal teams.
You will need: For each team - a supply of balloons, half filled with water.
The game:
Teams sit in relay form and the first two in each team make up a traditional 'wheelbarrow', with player 1 being the barrow and player 2 the pusher. The barrow holds the balloon between his or her teeth and, on the word 'Go', must race up to a given point and back again. Player 2 becomes the barrow with player 3 the pusher, and so on until the last player and the first have had their go together. Points are awarded for first, second and third - and deducted for each balloon burst.

56 - WATER PYRAMIDS

Number of players: Any.
You will need: A good supply
of plastic cups and water.
The game:
Working on their own or
in pairs, players build
a pyramid using the cups
filled with water.
See how high they build them
- and see the effect of
pouring water gently into
the top cup.

41

57 - CHIN PASS

Number of players: Any, in equal teams.
You will need: For each team - a sponge and a supply of water.
The game:
Teams line up in relay form, with the wet sponge at one end. On the word 'Go', the sponge is placed under the chin of player 1 and then passed to player 2, who must only use his or her chin to grab the sponge - hands are not permitted. The sponge continues down the line until it gets to the last person. The sponge is then resoaked and passed back up the line. First team to finish is the winner.

58 - BIN BUNDLE

Number of players: Any, in equal teams.
You will need: For each team - a plastic dustbin liner and a good supply of water.
The game:
Teams are shown a course and are given a dustbin liner, as full as possible with water. On the word 'Go', each team must negotiate its bag of water around the course, as quickly as possible. Teams are given points for their order of finishing, and for the quantity of water remaining in their dustbin liners.

59 - WET SACK RACE

Number of players: Any, in equal teams.
You will need: For each team - a cloth sack, mug, empty bucket and a bowl of water.
The game:
Teams line up in relay form and, on the word 'Go', the first player in each team gets into the sack, fills the mug with water and must hop to their bucket, whereupon any water left in the mug is emptied into the bucket. Players return to their teams and set off the next in line. Award points for finishing, and for the amount of water collected.

60 - HEADS TOGETHER

Number of players: Any, in equal teams.
You will need: For each team - a sponge and a bowl of water.
The game:
Teams line up in relay form and, on the word 'Go', players 1 and 2 in each line place the wet sponge between their foreheads. They race, facing each other, to a given point and back again, where the sponge is resoaked and player 2 runs with player 3, then 3 and 4, 4 and 5, 5 and 1. When all have run twice, award points for order of finishing and the amount of water collected.

61 - THREE-LEGGED CHAOS

Number of players: Any, in equal teams.
You will need: For each team - a mug, empty bucket and a bowl of water, plus something to tie two legs together.
The game:
Teams line up in relay form and, on the word 'Go', players 1 and 2 in each line pair up and tie one of each of their legs together. One of the pair fills the mug with water and they race to the bucket where they empty the mug. They run back to their team, remove the rope (or whatever) from their legs and player 2 pairs up with player 3, then 3 and 4, 4 and 5, 5 and 1. When all have run twice, award points for order of finishing and the amount of water collected.

62 - OVER THE TOP

Number of players: Any, in teams.
You will need: A large groundsheet, a length of rope from which to suspend it and various cups and billies.
The activity:
The groundsheet is suspended curtain-like across the playing area. Teams are given a measured quantity of water and, using what implements and initiative they can muster, transfer their water from one side of the curtain to the other. The two large water containers must not leave the ground. Either complete this as a race, against the clock or simply to see how much water can be retained.

63 - PIPELINE

Number of players: Any, in teams.
You will need: A large supply of plastic drinking straws and a small supply of water.
The activity:
Teams are given a jug of water and a bundle of straws and have 15 minutes or so in which to build a watertight pipeline to cover as long a distance as possible. Test it by pouring water through it using a funnel of paper, and by making team members lie down and hold the pipeline above them.

64 - WATER CONSERVATION

Number of players: Any, in teams.
You will need: All sorts of things!
The activity:
This activity takes place over, say, an evening's group meeting of an hour or so and involves the teams being issued with a measured quantity of water (say, four litres) at the start and seeing how much they have left at the end. A variety of games from the pages of this book could be used, such as nos: 2, 8, 11, 14, 22, 25, 44, 58, 59, 60, 61, and activities such as PIPELINE (64) and OVER THE TOP (65) could easily be incorporated. Award points for each activity and deduct points at the end of the evening for any water lost.

65 - SQUARE BOMBING

Number of players: At least 15.
You will need: A supply of balloons, partly filled with water.
The game:
A square playing area is marked, with the players standing within it. Four attackers stand around the square, one of whom has a balloon, which is thrown at the defending players. If it touches them, or if it bursts and they get wet, players are out and must leave the square. If a player in the square catches the balloon, the first player to be out rejoins the game. This continues for a given time, say, ten minutes.

66 - HEADS 'N' HANDS

Number of players: Ten or more.
You will need: A sponge football and a bowl or two of water.
The game:
Players stand in a large circle with a leader standing in the centre. The leader passes the water-soaked ball to each player in turn with the command 'Heads' or 'Hands' said by the leader as soon as the ball is thrown. If 'Heads' is said, the player must catch the ball and pass it back to the leader. If 'Hands', the player heads it back. An incorrect action means the player is out and sits down or gains a penalty point. The ball should be recharged with water from time to time - and the leader should either be content to get wet or wear a good cagoule or raincoat!

67 - YOGI DUNKING

Number of players: Any, in equal teams.
You will need: For each team - items as for either JELLY
DUNKING or MALTESER DUNKING, plus a plate of flour
in which are buried several wine gums or similar sweets.
The game:
This is played as both JELLY DUNKING and MALTESER
DUNKING, but players must visit the bowl of water first, eat a
sweet and then on to the plate of flour. Again, without using
hands, they must try to locate a sweet before running back to
the team. A towel for each team might be a useful addition -
as well as a camera to record the Yogi Bear lookalikes!

68 - LOTTA BOTTLE

Number of players: Any, in equal teams.
You will need: For each team - an empty milk bottle, a bowl of water and a dishcloth.
The game:
Teams line up in relay formation, with the bowl of water and dishcloth at the front of each team. One person is selected from each team and he or she must lie down some distance directly in front of his or her team (about 12-15 metres away). These players must hold the milk bottle on their stomachs. On the word 'Go', the first player in each team grabs their dishcloth, soaks it in water and runs up to their friend with the bottle. They must squeeze as much water into the bottle as they can and then run back to set the next player in their team off. After a given time (say, four minutes), the game is stopped and whichever team has the fullest bottle is the winner. If the bottle is filled, it may be emptied and the quantity noted by the referee.

69 - LOTTA BOTTLE STRIKES BACK!

Number of players: Any, in equal teams.
You will need: For each team - a blindfold, an empty milk bottle, a bowl of water and a plastic cup.
The game:
This is played as in LOTTA BOTTLE, except that a plastic cup replaces the dishcloth, and the runners must be blindfolded before they set off (and a shorter course is suggested). The player with the bottle must guide their team mate to them by shouting directions. The player with the bottle must not move as he or she verbally directs the blindfolded one to pour the water into the bottle. A judge with each team should keep a note of the water collected. The game continues until each player has had a turn.